Encyclopedia of
Legendary Creatures

Encyclopedia of
Legendary Creatures

By Tom McGowen
Illustrated by Victor G. Ambrus

Rand McNally & Company
Chicago · New York · San Francisco

For Brian and Blake

Library of Congress Cataloging in Publication Data

McGowen, Tom.
 Encyclopedia of legendary creatures.

 Summary: Presents, in encyclopedia format, monsters and supernatural
beings from Abominable Snowman to Zombi.
 1. Fairies—Dictionaries, Juvenile. 2. Animals, Mythical—Dictionaries,
Juvenile. 3. Monsters—Dictionaries, Juvenile. 4. Dwarfs —Dictionaries,
Juvenile. [1. Monsters— Dictionaries. 2. Fairies—Dictionaries. 3. Animals,
Mythical—Dictionaries. 4. Folklore—Dictionaries] I. Ambrus, Victor G., ill.
II. Title.
GR550.M35   398.2′454′03   81-10529
ISBN 0-528-82402-3   AACR2
ISBN 0-528-80074-4 (lib. bdg.)

First printing, 1981

Author's Note

The creatures presented in this book are things people once believed in and, in some cases, still do. They do not include any deities that were actually worshipped (gods and goddesses), any of the animal culture heroes (such as Coyote and Hare), or any strictly tall-tale characters (such as Paul Bunyan). Rather, they fall into the category of monsters and supernatural beings that were usually either feared (such as Ogres and Dragons) or simply accepted as a fact of life (such as Brownies and Unicorns). A few of them may actually have existed once, and a few of them may actually exist now. Most, however, are merely figments of humankind's fertile imagination or real things or people that became distorted into monsters and supernatural beings by the passage of time and the art of storytellers.

The coverage of these creatures is by no means complete; a simple listing of all the beings of myth, legend, and folklore from every land and every age would run to thousands of names. For example, nearly every group of people in the world has, or had, legends of the little men we call Dwarfs, all known by different names. It has been my intent merely to provide a sizeable cross-section of the many sorts of marvelous creatures that people all over the world shivered over and wondered about, probably for thirty thousand years and more.

Tom McGowen

Abatwa

A

Abatwa People

Among the Zulu people of South Africa, tales were told of men who suddenly heard a shrill voice speaking to them from the ground. Looking down, the man would see a tiny, tiny figure standing near his feet and would know he had met one of the Abatwa People.

The Abatwa were the smallest people in the world. They slept in anthills and walked among blades of grass as full-sized people walk among trees in a forest. But they were very self-conscious about their size, and if a man met an Abatwa, he had to be very careful to pretend the little creature was a full-sized person. Otherwise, the Abatwa would become enraged and shoot at the man with tiny poisoned arrows!

Abiku

In the West African country of the Yoruba people, it was once believed that children were in constant danger. For, it was known that the land was haunted by dreadful, evil spirits known as Abiku, who roamed in search of children whose bodies they sought to take over. And for a child to become possessed by an Abiku meant death!

The Abiku were shapeless, ghostlike things. Having no bodies, they of course had no stomachs; yet they were always dreadfully hungry and thirsty. The only way they might appease their hunger and thirst was by entering a child's body, for then everything the child ate and drank would go to nourish the Abiku within. But the child would slowly waste away and die.

So, Yoruba parents watched their children for signs of an Abiku. If a child began to get thin and weak, even though well fed, the parents knew the young one was possessed. Then there was only one thing to do: They had to make cuts in the child's skin and rub the cuts with pepper. The pain would drive out the Abiku and the child would be saved.

Abominable Snowman, or Yeti

The jet black sky is spangled with thousands of glittering stars. The snowy mountainside glistens in the moonlight. Suddenly, through the night's cold stillness drifts a distant, high-pitched whistling. Hearing this sound, the people in remote settlements of this mountainous land shudder with fear, for they know the Abominable Snowman is abroad.

Tibet, Nepal, Bhutan, and Sikkim lie high in the Himalaya Mountains between India and China. For centuries, the people of these lands have told of tall, furry, humanlike creatures that live in caves near the mountaintops and prowl the snow-covered mountainsides by night. The people of Tibet call these creatures Metoh-kangmi, or, "Abominable Snowmen." (*Abominable* means "hateful" or "disgusting.") In Nepal, the creatures

are known as Yetis, meaning "all-devouring things."

At night, sounds said to be those of Abominable Snowmen—a high-pitched whistling noise or a loud mewing or sometimes angry roars—are sometimes heard echoing among the mountains. The Abominable Snowmen are believed to be meat eaters who hunt the big, shaggy, oxlike creatures called yaks as well as little rabbitlike pikas. It is also claimed that Abominable Snowmen sometimes raid villages and carry off people for food!

Abominable Snowmen have a strong, disgusting odor that can be smelled far off. These creatures are extremely strong and can pull up trees by the roots and throw large, heavy boulders great distances. They have pointed heads and long, thick hair. Tibetan children know that the best way to escape an Abominable Snowman is to run straight downhill, for when the creature tries to follow, its long hair will fall into its eyes, making it unable to see.

Explorers and mountain climbers from England, Australia, and other countries have seen huge footprints in the snow and were told these were tracks of Abominable Snowmen. In 1925, a well-known British explorer saw a distant, dark, humanlike form walking in the snow on a mountainside and later found strange tracks. However, no Abominable Snowman has ever been captured or even photographed, and several scientific expeditions that searched for these creatures were unable to find any evidence that Abominable Snowmen really exist. Skins and scalps said to be those of Abominable Snowmen turned out to be from ordinary animals.

Acheri

Many North American Indian tribes knew of the Acheri. It lived on a mountaintop and looked like a thin, pale, little girl. At night, it would come down from the mountain to dance, to sing wailing songs, and to bring trouble and sorrow to humans—for the Acheri was a spirit of sickness and death. When a child became ill, parents knew the Acheri had cast its shadow upon the little one. The Acheri, however, would not harm anyone who wore red, so Indian mothers often tied red strings around the necks of their children to protect them.

Ahuizotl

The Aztec people of Mexico greatly feared the Ahuizotl. It dwelt in the deep waters of a lake, and

Abominable Snowman

anyone approaching the lake's edge was in dreadful danger. The Ahuizotl's tail—an enormously long tail with a *hand* on the end—might come sliding out of the dark water to drag the person into the depths! Three days later, the drowned person's body would be found cast back up onto shore, with eyes, teeth, and fingernails missing, taken by the Ahuizotl for some strange purpose of its own.

The Ahuizotl often lured people to their doom. It could make frogs and fish jump in the water, so that a fisherman might come hurrying with his net, eager to make a catch. Sometimes the Ahuizotl cried with the voice of a child, so that some man or woman would come to see if a child were in trouble.

It was said that even if someone managed to escape the Ahuizotl's clutching tail, he or she would soon die anyway. And it was said that any person who actually saw the Ahuizotl would die of fright!

Aigamuchab

The Aigamucha were a race of strange and dangerous creatures said to live in villages in the Kalahari Desert of southwestern Africa. In most ways they were like humans—but they had pointed teeth as long as a person's finger, and their eyes were on the insteps of their feet! Thus, when they walked upright, they were always looking straight up at the sky. If an Aigamuchab wanted to see what was going on around him, he got down on his hands and knees and held one foot so that the eye on that foot could see ahead and held the other so that its eye could look behind.

Humans, known as the Nama people, also lived in the Kalahari. These people feared they might be hunted by the fierce Aigamucha, who would tear them to pieces with their terrible teeth. But the Nama people also knew they had only to throw powdered tobacco on the ground if they were pursued. The tobacco dust would get into the eyes on the Aigamucha's feet, stinging and blinding them so that the Nama people could escape.

Al

Als were half-human, half-animal creatures feared by the people of Armenia, a mountainous land that is now part of the Soviet Union. Als lived in damp, watery places or sometimes lurked in the corners of stables. They were shaggy, with fiery eyes and snaky hair. Their teeth were iron and their fingernails were brass.

Als were most dangerous to women who were about to have babies, for the Als delighted in causing a baby to be born blind or deformed. To keep the dreadful creatures away, a woman had to carry an iron weapon or tool and had to sleep

Al

surrounded by iron objects. But even if a baby was born safely, an Al might wait until the baby was seven months old; then it would steal the child from its cradle and carry it off to the Al king to be eaten!

Ankou

When people of Brittany, on the coast of France, heard the sound of distant, creaking cart wheels at night, they knew it might mean the Ankou was abroad. The Ankou was said to look like a tall, gaunt man with a pale face and long white hair. He drove a cart drawn by a pale, bony horse. Beside the cart walked two silent figures.

People knew that when the Ankou's cart stopped at a house, someone in the house would die. The two figures with the Ankou would pace solemnly into the house and return carrying a body. They then placed the body in the cart, and the Ankou would drive off into the darkness, the sound of his cart's wheels fading into the distance.

Arwe

Long ago, the land of Ethiopia was ruled by Arwe, an enormous serpent whose body was long as a river, whose teeth were long as a man's arm, and whose skin was like iron. Arwe ate up the people's sheep, goats, and cattle, until hardly any were left and people were starving. He then demanded that the prettiest girls in the land be served to him as food. Arwe was finally killed by a man who fed him a bowl of poison, telling him it was goat's milk.

Azeman

In Surinam, a little country in South America, people dreaded the Azeman—a combination of werewolf and vampire! An Azeman was an ordinary woman by day, but at night she would take the form of an animal and prowl through the darkness in search of a victim whose blood she might drink!

But there were ways of keeping an Azeman out of a house. If a broom was propped across the doorway, the Azeman couldn't pass it. And if a quantity of rice or pepper was scattered on the ground, the Azeman was compelled to stop and count every grain or speck. If she was still counting when the sun rose, she would resume her human form and could be captured.

B

Baba Yaga

Somewhere in a clearing in a Russian forest was a little hut which, instead of standing on the ground, was perched on four chicken legs. The hut was surrounded by a picket fence, and stuck on each picket was a human skull! This was the home of the dreaded ogress Baba Yaga.

Baba Yaga looked like a frightfully ugly old woman. She had stone teeth, and her food was people, especially children, whom she captured and then cooked in a big pot. She was a powerful magician and flew through the air after her prey in a large mortar, steered with a pestle.

Banshee

It was a dark night in Ireland. Ragged clouds drifted across a moonless sky. Wind rippled the tall grass in the meadows.

Suddenly, a frightful sound was heard. It began as a low moan, rising into a long, wailing shriek that slowly faded away into a sob. It was the wail of a Banshee—and it meant that death was coming for someone!

A Banshee was heard, and perhaps seen, only when someone was soon to die. It appeared as a beautiful weeping woman in a long, green gown and a gray cloak. Her eyes were red from weeping, and as she wailed, she tore her hair in grief.

Baba Yaga

of a toad. It wasn't very big—only about the size of a cat—but it was the most deadly of all creatures. Any plant it breathed upon would wither and die, any rock it touched would split, and any animal or human that even saw it would drop dead. The very sound it made—an evil hissing—could sometimes cause death!

Everyone knew that a Basilisk should be killed as soon as it hatched, but obviously, killing one wasn't easy. It was believed that the best way was to place a mirror where the Basilisk might come upon it suddenly. When the creature saw itself in the mirror, it would drop dead. But even a dead Basilisk was dangerous, for it was said that merely touching its lifeless body could cause a person to sicken and die.

The Basilisk was also known as a Cockatrice.

Banshees usually only wailed to foretell the deaths of members of the old or noble families of Ireland—people whose names began with *O*, *Mc*, or *Mac*.

Basilisk

People of the Middle Ages believed that once in a great while, when the positions of the stars were just right, a seven-year-old male chicken—a rooster—would lay an egg. Then, along would come a snake, to coil around the egg, or a toad, to squat upon the egg, keeping it warm and helping it hatch. When it hatched, out came a fearful creature called a Basilisk.

A Basilisk had the body, wings, and feet of a rooster, the head and tail of a snake, and the eyes

Basilisk

Bay-kok

Bay-kok was a horrible creature who roamed the forest in the land of the Chippewa Indian people. He was a skeleton with glowing red eyes and covered with a thin, transparent skin. He carried a bow and arrows and a war club, for he was a hunter—but what he hunted was men!

Bay-kok came to the forest from the east each spring and moved slowly westward until the end of autumn. As he walked, his bones rattled, and Chippewa hunters, hearing a rattling noise in the woods at night, knew Bay-kok was passing and someone would soon die. For when Bay-kok came upon a sleeping hunter, he would squat down and cut a tiny opening in the man's chest—so gently that the sleeper never awoke. He would then remove a small bit of the man's stomach and eat it. The man never knew what happened, but before long he would waste away and die.

Bay-kok

Bigfoot

Indians of the northwestern part of North America told tales of huge, shaggy humanlike creatures living in the deep forests of the mountain country. These creatures were known to the Indians as Sasquatch or Seeahtik. It was said they could make themselves invisible and had other strange powers.

In 1924, some miners who had been working in a canyon in Washington State claimed they shot and wounded a big, gorillalike creature and later were attacked by a number of similar creatures. A man who camped in western Canada that same year claimed he was held prisoner for a time by a group of four hairy humanlike things that were from seven to eight feet tall.

Over a period of many years, numerous other people claimed to have seen creatures such as these. Also, many huge, humanlike footprints have been found, as much as sixteen inches long and seven inches wide. Because of these footprints, the unknown creature became known as Bigfoot.

Bigfoot is said to walk upright on two legs, like a human, but in a slow, shuffling way. Its shoulders are wide and powerful and it has hardly any neck. Its face is apelike, and there is long hair on its head, forming bangs on its forehead. Bigfoot's body is covered with hair that is usually reddish, but may also be black, tan, or white. The creature apparently eats only plant food and does not seem to be dangerous to humans unless they try to hurt it.

No Bigfoot has ever been captured, and no skeletons of anything like a Bigfoot have ever been found. Because of this, most scientists feel that Bigfoot does not really exist and is only a legend. However, a few scientists think there may well be such creatures and that they are a kind of ape.

Black Annis

Black Annis lived in a cave in the rugged highlands of Scotland. She was a hideous hag with blue skin and only one eye. She generally sat outside her cave beside a gigantic pile of the bones of things she had eaten—and the bones of anyone who chanced to come near her would soon be added to the pile! However, Black Annis's favorite food was strayed lambs and lost children, for which she kept an eager watch with her one eye.

Black Dog

An Englishman walking along a lonely country road at night might suddenly become aware of a large, four-footed shape, blacker than the night's

blackness, trotting alongside him at the road's edge. The man might catch a gleam of fiery red eyes as the creature glanced sidelong at him. Then he would know he was in the company of a Black Dog—one of the strange, shaggy, black, glowing-eyed creatures, large as a calf or pony, that are

Bigfoot

sometimes seen in many parts of the English countryside at night.

If the man knew about Black Dogs—as most English countrypeople still do—he would just keep on walking, never uttering a word and not even looking toward the shape, and he wouldn't be harmed. But, woe betide the person who tries to talk to a Black Dog, or, worse yet, tries to touch one. It is said that person will be struck senseless and will die soon after!

Blue Men of the Minch

The Minch is a stretch of sea, about thirty miles wide, between the west coast of Scotland and one of the Hebrides Islands. When the weather over the Minch was stormy, the captain of a ship making its way through those waters knew he had best beware, for the Blue Men were up and about.

The Blue Men lived in the water. They looked like ordinary men, but their skins were blue. Whenever they were asleep, the weather was fine, but when they awoke, the weather turned stormy. And if a ship came through the Minch when the Blue Men were awake, they would come swimming to do their best to wreck it.

Clever Scottish sea captains, however, usually knew how to best the Blue Men. When a captain saw the blue-skinned creatures sliding through the water toward his ship, he would call out to them. If he could talk to them quickly and cleverly in rhyme, never letting them have the last word, they had no power, and his ship could pass through the Minch in safety.

Bodach

Bodachs lived in Scotland and looked like very small, shriveled-up old men. Scottish children knew that if they became too naughty, a Bodach might come get them some night! It would creep down through the chimney of the house and steal

Black Dog

the child right out of his or her bed. And a child taken by a Bodach was never seen again.

Bogeyman—*see* Goblin

Brownie

Boggart

Many a deep black hole in England once had its Boggart. They were mischievous creatures, fond of playing tricks on people—such as moving all a house's furniture around at night. But if a Boggart became angry at someone, its tricks might turn destructive. It might break all a person's dishes, spill all the milk, and turn the cows and horses loose to wander off and get lost.

No one knew exactly what a Boggart looked like, for the creatures could apparently take different forms if they wished. But they seemed to prefer doing their mischief on dark, cloudy nights, for an old English poem says:

> Stars are shining, moon is bright.
> Boggart won't come out tonight.

Boggarts don't bother people much anymore. It is said that they now spend most of their time hiding from automobiles, of which they are terrified.

Brownie

Scottish families lucky enough to have a Brownie living near them were lucky indeed. For although Brownies were ugly creatures—tiny, shaggy men with noses that were no more than two holes— they seemed to delight in doing things for people. A Brownie might creep into a house at night to sweep the floor, wash dirty dishes, and churn the butter. However, Brownies seemed to get annoyed if a house was so tidy there was nothing for them to do, for then they would mess things up!

Brownies wouldn't take pay for the help they gave, but people often left out a bowl of milk and bits of bread as if by accident, and a Brownie would gladly gobble up this food. But people who tried to do *too* much for a Brownie, such as leaving out some clothes for him, would simply drive him away.

Bunyip

Bunyip

Bunyips were rather mysterious and dangerous creatures said to live in waterholes, lakes, and rivers in Australia. There were apparently several different kinds. The Bunyip of Lake Alexandria was half-man and half-fish, with hair like a tangle of wet reeds. A Eumeralla River Bunyip was a big, brown creature with a long neck, a head like a kangaroo, a hairy mane, and an enormous mouth. But most Bunyips were said to have a furry body about the size of a large dog, webbed feet, and a doglike head.

Bunyips often bellowed in a terrible voice that could be heard for miles. If they could, they would pull people into the water and drown them.

Centaur

Centaurs were half-human, half-horse beings said to live in Thessaly, in ancient Greece. A Centaur had the body and four legs of a horse, but where the horse's neck and head should have been, there was the body of a man from the waist up. Thus, Centaurs had the speed and strength of a horse, combined with the intelligence and the skillful hands of a human.

Some Centaurs were on friendly terms with people. Others were wild, unruly creatures that often got into battles with humans.

Chimera

According to legend, the Chimera was a monster that lived long ago in a country known as Lycia, in the Near East. The front part of its body resembled a lion; its middle section resembled a goat; and its back part looked like a scaly, snaky dragon. The beast had three heads: that of a lion, a goat, and a dragon. Each head could shoot flames from its mouth.

The Chimera terrorized Lycia for a long time. It was finally killed by a young hero named Bellerophon.

Centaur

Clurican

A Clurican was a creature that looked like a shriveled-up, little old man. He lived in the cellar of an Irish house or inn, where the barrels of wine, beer, and whiskey were kept. After a human had come down to fill a glass or mug from a barrel, the Clurican made sure that the spigot on the barrel hadn't been left open so that liquid would trickle out and be wasted. In payment for this valuable work, the innkeeper or homeowner usually left a small supper in the cellar each night for the Clurican. It was said that every Clurican knew the whereabouts of a hidden treasure.

Cockatrice—see Basilisk

Cyclops

People of ancient Greece knew of the Cyclopes, a race of giants shaped like humans except that each Cyclops had only one eye in the center of its forehead. They were wild, savage creatures who lived in caves on an island and kept herds of giant goats and sheep.

On a day long ago, the ships of the Greek leader Odysseus came to the rocky coast of the land of the Cyclopes. Odysseus and some of his men explored for a time and came upon a cave that belonged to Polyphemus, one of the Cyclopes. While they were in the cave, the giant returned. He drove his sheep into the cave, then sealed up the entrance with a huge boulder, trapping the Greeks inside.

When Polyphemus saw the men, he promptly ate two of them, bones and all, and informed the others he would eat them as well. Odysseus, however, had brought along a container of wine and offered it to the giant. Polyphemus soon fell into a drunken slumber. Odysseus then burned a point onto the end of the giant's club and stabbed Polyphemus in the eye, blinding him.

Cyclops

The blind Cyclops groped about in the cave, but the men easily dodged him. So Polyphemus pushed the boulder aside and crouched at the entrance, waiting to grab and crush anyone who tried to get out. But the Greeks managed to escape by clinging to the undersides of the giant sheep; for as the sheep went past him, Polyphemus merely felt their wooly backs and let them go. And so, the Greeks were able to get back to their ships and sail away from the land of the terrible Cyclopes.

D

Dogai

"Behave, or the Dogai will come get you," Melanesian mothers on islands in the South Pacific Ocean once would say to naughty children. And the children would behave, for they were very much afraid of the Dogai. Dogai looked like hideous women with long, skinny legs and enormous ears—so enormous that when one of these creatures slept, she used one ear for a bed and the other as a blanket! The Dogai could make themselves look like animals, trees, rocks, and even groups of stars in the sky. They could also make themselves appear as beautiful women, and in this form, they would sometimes lure boys and girls away from their houses and then kill them.

Dog-headed People

The Estonians of long ago knew there were Dog-headed People living at the end of the world—a wild, unknown place just beyond the land of the Estonians. These creatures were said to have the bodies of men and women, but the heads of dogs. Each had a single large eye in the middle of its forehead. Dog-heads ran on all fours, as dogs do.

The Dog-heads were greatly feared by the Estonians, for it was believed that bands of the crea-

tures attacked villages, killing and eating the men and taking women and children captive. The captives were taken to Dog-head villages and kept much as humans keep sheep or cattle, to be fattened up and slaughtered for food as needed!

Domovoi

In every home in old Russia there was always a Domovoi. He was the very spirit of the house itself. In daytime, he stayed in the shadows under the stove or in the darkness under the steps of the front door. At night, he usually came out to look around and see that everyone and everything in the house was all right.

Domovoi

18

The Domovoi tried to avoid being seen, but Russians knew he generally looked like a very small man completely covered with silky fur, even to the palms of his hands. At times, he might look like a stray dog or cat, or perhaps like a bundle of hay someone had left in a corner.

In addition to looking after the house, a Domovoi would warn the family if trouble was coming. They would hear him groaning or sighing. If they heard him weeping, they knew one of them was going to die.

Dragon

Dragons were known in legends throughout most of the world. They were enormous reptiles, often with magical powers and the ability to talk. But they varied greatly in different parts of the world.

In Europe, there were tales of several kinds of Dragons. The kind known as a Worm resembled a gigantic snake, sometimes with four legs. A Firedrake was a four-legged cave Dragon, often with batlike wings. A Wyvern was also winged, but had only two legs. The Dragons of Europe usually lived in caves in forests or rocky, mountainous places. There, they lay upon piles of treasure they had stolen and gathered together over many years.

Courageous and daring men would sometimes try to overcome a Dragon and gain its treasure, but this was far from easy. Not only were most Dragons gigantic in size, but their scaly skins were hard as armor, and some of them could shoot blasts of fire from their mouth or nose. Dragons were also cunning and could often enchant a man with their conversation, lulling and soothing him until they suddenly struck.

A Dragon would sometimes beseige a city or ravage a countryside. The only way to keep a Dragon from eventually killing everyone and destroying everything was to give it a sacrifice— usually a young, beautiful princess—or to find a warrior who could kill it. Some especially strong and courageous warriors did manage to kill Drag-

Dragon

ons, saving a princess from death or gaining the Dragon's horde of treasure.

The Dragons of China were quite different from those of Europe. They were seldom if ever winged. They had long, scaly, snakelike bodies, and their heads were somewhat like the head of a horse, but with whiskers and a pair of antlerlike horns. Unlike the wild, savage Dragons of Europe, Chinese Dragons were highly civilized and had their own kingdom with a government and laws. And unlike the troublesome European Dragons, Chinese Dragons were generally kind and helpful to humans. They often appeared in human form, usually as a man with a very large mouth, a green beard, and Dragon horns sprouting from his head.

See: Arwe; Fafnir; Lambton Worm; Tarasque.

Dwarf

There are legends of Dwarfs in all parts of the world, but Dwarfs played an especially big role in the legends of Germany, Sweden, and other northern lands. The northern Dwarfs were said to resemble old, wrinkled, rather ugly men and women, often with humped backs and too-large heads. Some of them had feet that were on backward; others had the webbed feet of a duck or goose. Dwarfs were believed to live underground or in the deepest parts of forests. They wore pointed red caps and garments of black, brown, and gray.

Male Dwarfs were reputed to be skilled makers of marvelous swords, helmets, and armor, as well as beautiful brooches, rings, cups, and other objects made of gold, silver, and precious stones. Dwarf women were supposedly skilled at the spinning and weaving of fine cloth and tapestries.

Most Dwarfs could do a bit of magic, such as making themselves invisible, or foretelling the future. Dwarfs and people usually got on well. The Dwarfs seemed willing to share their greater

knowledge with humans, and it was said that Dwarfs had first shown humans how to bake, how to make clothing, and how to make things of metal.

Dwarfs were apparently long-lived, but they grew old early. They were full-grown by the age of three, and male Dwarfs had long gray beards by the time they were seven.

Dwarfs

20

E

Elf

Elves were very small, humanlike beings that, like Dwarfs, played a large part in the legends of Germany, Sweden, Denmark, and Norway. There, they were known as Alfar or Alvor. Later, they were transported to England, Scotland, and Ireland, where they became known as Elves.

There were two kinds of Elves: Elves of Light and Elves of Darkness. The Elves of Light were known to be gay, mischievous creatures who dwelt in a bright, enchanted realm filled with gardens and the sound of music. The women were dainty and beautiful, and the men were sturdy and handsome. But Elves of Darkness looked like small misshapen people. They lived in a lightless underground region and could not come above the ground in daylight or they would be turned to stone. The men usually wore leather aprons and carried lanterns, picks, and shovels for their work as miners. They were marvelous craftsmen and artists who made beautiful objects out of gold, silver, and jewels.

Elves of Light often held festivals and dances in forests and meadows during the hours of darkness, whisking back to their magic land when they heard the first morning crow of a rooster. Any human who happened to come upon a group of dancing Elves was in danger of being enchanted and carried off to Elfland or of becoming the victim of mischievous Elf pranks. Elf women delighted in bewitching mortal men; they were jealous of human brides and would steal their husbands if they could.

Elves of Darkness were also fond of playing tricks on humans. A favorite trick was to stalk humans in a lonely place and frighten them by echoing their voices. Thus, many people believed any echo was an Elf of Darkness, mocking them.

Elves

F

Fafnir

In a cave on a wooded mountainside, Fafnir lay slumbering upon a pile of golden treasure. He was a great, scaled, wingless dragon of the kind known as a Worm to the ancient Norse people.

Fafnir had murdered his own father to get the treasure he now guarded. He was actually the son of Hreidmar, king of the Dwarfs, and he had once been a Dwarf. But, when Hreidmar had received the mass of gold from the gods, Fafnir had killed him, taken the gold to the cave, and become a dragon by enchantment. Now, day after day and year after year, Fafnir lay in darkness upon the cold metal, snuffing and licking it hungrily.

But, one day, a young hero named Sigurd came to the cave. Quickly, Sigurd dug a shallow trench just outside the cave entrance. Lying down in the trench, he called out a challenge.

Roaring in fury, Fafnir came forth. But he did not see Sigurd, and as he strode over the trench, Sigurd thrust his sword upward, driving it deep

Fafnir

22

into the dragon's heart. Thus, Fafnir died and the treasure passed into Sigurd's hands.

Fairy

Fairies have long been known as supernatural beings that live in another world separate from, but joined to, the earth. Many legends say that Fairies often came to earth and sometimes had dealings with humans.

Many of the Fairies of England, Ireland, Scotland, and Wales were said to look like tall, very handsome men and women. They were usually dressed in white or shining clothing. Their hair was often fair (blond), and in Wales they were known as the Fair Family.

In Ireland there are many large mounds of earth, known as shees, built thousands of years ago and said to be entrances to the Fairy world. Humans were sometimes taken or invited into Fairyland, which seemed to be an incredibly beautiful place where the Fairies spent their time riding on windswift white horses, hunting with packs of snow white hounds, and feasting on marvelously delicious foods in their glittering palaces. This may all have been just an illusion, however. A few humans in Fairyland rubbed a magical ointment into their eyes and saw that the place actually seemed to be a dismal cavern, the food was only leaves and moldy grain, and the Fairies were thin and starved-looking. Anything that was brought out of Fairyland by a human always changed shape; gold coins turned into dried leaves, and food became garbage. Humans who had been in Fairyland also found that many years or even centuries had passed while they were there, for half an hour in Fairyland was equal to a year upon earth.

Some kinds of Fairies were small—no bigger than very young children—or even only a few inches high. Some of these were dainty and beautiful little people, sometimes with gauzy, insectlike wings, but others were ugly and deformed. Most of these little Fairies, like the big ones, were fond of music and merriment and often came to earth at night to dance in meadows and forest glades. People could often tell where Fairies had danced by the presence of a Fairy Ring—a large circle of grass, greener than the rest, usually surrounded by a ring of toadstools.

Both big and little Fairies could be troublesome and even dangerous to humans. Some of them delighted in playing mischievous tricks on people, and some were deliberately cruel. At times, Fairies would steal a human baby and leave one of their own young—a changeling—in the human child's cradle. Fairies also took humans, usually women, captive and made them into servants. Such women were kidnapped out of their beds at night, and a magical, lifelike dummy was left in the woman's place to fool her husband or family. The dummy would seem to become sick, die, and would then be buried. The sorrowing husband or family would never know that the woman was actually still alive, a captive in Fairyland.

Fairies were said to live forever and could not be

Fairies

killed. They could, however, be kept away from humans by means of objects made of iron—the presence of which was painful to them—or by certain magic spells. If sprinkled with holy water, Fairies would vanish.

Fay

Fays were fairies that looked like human women. When a baby was born to the wife of a king or other great noble, Fays would often bestow magical gifts upon the child. Good Fays were usually beautiful and bestowed lifelong good luck on the baby. But there were also evil Fays, who might bring bad luck. It was a wicked Fay who caused the princess known as Sleeping Beauty to fall into her slumber. Fays apparently lived all together on a magical isle.

Fenris

Fenris or Fenrir was a gigantic wolf, so huge that when he opened his mouth, his lower jaw scraped the earth, while his nose touched the sky. According to legend, Fenris was a creature of evil, and the Norse gods had made him a captive, binding him with magical chains made by dwarfs. But, it was known that there would someday be an earth-shattering war between the forces of good and evil.

On that day, Fenris would break his chains and rush to the battlefield with fire spurting from his eyes and blood dripping from his giant jaws.

Fomorians

The Fomorians were a race of evil, misshapen giants who ruled Ireland in legendary times. Some Fomorians had the head of an animal. Others had only one arm, or one leg, or no feet. Their king Balor had only one eye, which could cause death to any living thing it looked upon.

The abode of the Fomorians was a grim, rocky island in the sea off the coast of Ireland. The Fomorians had power over the sea and could cause darkness, fog, and storms. They could also cause disease to strike people and could make crops wither and die.

The people of Ireland lived in terror of these creatures. Finally, however, the Irish rose up and fought a great battle against their oppressors. The power of the Fomorians was broken, and the giants fled into the sea, never to be seen again.

Fenris

G

Ghost

In all parts of the world there is a belief that when some people die, a part of them remains alive in spirit form as a creature that is called a Ghost, Shade, Phantom, or Spectre.

In most Ghost tales, a Ghost is never solid and may often be invisible. However, even when it can be seen, a Ghost has no substance and can pass through walls and other solid things. Some kinds of Ghosts are said to look just as the person did when alive; others look like the person did when he or she was buried. Some Ghosts are merely formless, drifting shapes. Ghosts are generally reputed to be seen only at night.

According to legend, some Ghosts are spirits of people who did great evil while they were alive and so must wander restlessly forever as punishment. Such Ghosts may be harmful to people. Many Hindus believe that a person who dies unhappy will also become a wandering, harmful Ghost.

Ghosts that haunt certain places are usually thought to be spirits of people who were murdered or buried in those places. They are seeking either to have their murderers punished or to have their bodies buried in a proper cemetery. In many tales, the Ghost of a friend or relative will appear to a person to warn of some coming disaster or to reveal where some important object, which has been lost, may be found.

Although Ghosts have no substance, they are often able to speak and sometimes have the power to move things and to cause people to feel certain sensations, such as extreme cold. Apparently, however, no Ghost can do physical harm, such as strangling or stabbing a person. But many people believe that a Ghost, through the sheer terror of its presence, can cause people to injure themselves or even to die of fright.

Ghoul

In ancient times, a group of Arabs traveling through a desert at night might see furtive, indistinct shapes flitting among the sand dunes in the darkness. The men would shiver and draw closer together for protection. They were being stalked by Ghouls!

Ghouls were dreadful, man-eating creatures that lived in the deserts of Arabia and North Africa.

Ghouls

Ghoul

lure some curious person into leaving the group and going into the desert alone. Or, a Ghoul might make itself look like a beautiful girl and appear to a lone man keeping watch at night while his comrades slept. If she succeeded in getting the man to leave his camp with her, he was doomed. Once Ghouls got the man alone, they would kill him and feast upon his flesh.

These creatures were particularly fond of young children as food. But they really weren't a bit particular. If they couldn't find a live human to kill and eat, they would go to a graveyard and dig up a corpse . . .

Giants

Giants were humanlike creatures of great size and strength found in the legends of all parts of the world. They ranged in size from only seven or eight feet tall to the height of a lofty mountain. Many Giants were simply extra-large men and women, but some were deformed monsters, often with a single eye or with several heads. Many were eaters of human flesh.

See: Cyclops; Fomorians; Gigantes; Goo-Teekhl; Jotunn; Khumbaba; Sasabonsam; Torch; Troll; Wendigo.

Gigantes

The Gigantes were a race of enormous giants that, according to the ancient Greeks, lived in the earliest days of the world. They had human bodies, but their feet were serpent tails. The Gigantes fought a great battle against the Greek gods and were defeated. One of them, Enceladus, is said to be buried alive beneath the island of Sicily, which the goddess Pallas Athene slammed down on him during the battle. So huge is he, the island barely covers him, and legend has it that the volcanic

They prowled by night, and the next day their hoofed footprints would be seen in the sand. Ghouls had no particular shape, and no one knew exactly what they looked like, as they could take on any shape they wished.

Ghouls roamed the desert watching for parties of travelers. They sometimes built fires, hoping to rumblings of Sicily's Mount Aetna are really Enceladus trying to push the island off himself.

Gnome

Gnomes looked like small, hideous, deformed men. They lived at the very center of the earth and could swim through solid rock as easily as fish swim through water. They felt that all things within the earth belonged to them, and they tried to prevent humans from digging up gold, silver, and other minerals. Gnomes also had the power to make humans feel sad. Their king was named Gob, and he possessed a magic sword.

Goblin

Goblins were small manlike creatures known in France and the British Isles. French Goblins were good-natured but inclined to be mischievous. Some of them enjoyed entering houses at night to startle people out of their sleep by pounding on walls or banging pots together. Others would attach themselves to a human family and make themselves useful by doing chores at night. These Goblins seemed to like children and actually helped take care of little ones, punishing them with tricks when they were naughty and rewarding them with little gifts when they were good.

The British Goblins were quite different. Some of them, known as Hobgoblins, were merely mischievous and not harmful. But the true Goblins of England were downright evil. They were hideous, misshapen things that lived in caves and in the depths of forests. They, too, were fond of children—to eat! British Goblins were also called Bogles, Bogeys, Bogeymen, Bugbears, and Bugaboos.

Golem

It is said that one night more than four hundred years ago, in the Polish town of Chelm, people saw

Gnomes

Goblins

a terrifying sight. Striding through the moonlit streets came a huge, silent figure. It moved stiffly, its eyes never blinked, and its face was expressionless. As it neared people, they saw with horror that it was made entirely of clay! A Golem!

A Golem was a statue of a man or woman made of clay or wood and brought to life with a magical formula called a shem, which was written on a piece of paper. When the paper was put into the Golem's mouth, the statue came to life. When the paper was removed, the Golem again became a lifeless statue.

Although a Golem could move and could perform tasks it was ordered to do, it could not actually think. It was really just a kind of magical machine that could do only what it was told. This could cause trouble. According to legend, one Golem, made in Russia, was ordered to build a fire. It built such a huge one that the whole town burned down! The Golem made in Chelm was said to have caused so much trouble it had to be destroyed.

Goo-Teekhl

Goo-Teekhl was a giant who lived in the land of the Tlingit Indian people, now part of Alaska. He raided villages, seizing people to feast on their flesh and drink their blood. It was impossible to kill him, for his heart was hidden in an unknown place.

But one day, a young Tlingit warrior learned that Goo-Teekhl kept his heart in his left heel. The warrior fired an arrow into the vital spot. With a shriek, Goo-Teekhl fell. But, as the giant lay dying, he boasted to the warrior, "Even if you burn me to ashes, I will still drink the blood of humans!"

Angered by the boast and determined to prove Goo-Teekhl a liar, the warrior built a fire and burned the giant's body to ashes. Suddenly, the ashes became mosquitoes—the first mosquitoes in the world. And, just as Goo-Teekhl had boasted, mosquitoes still drink the blood of humans.

Gorgon

Gorgons were ugly, deadly beasts said to have lived in Africa long ago. A Gorgon was about the

Gorgon

size and shape of a bull, but it had large, thick scales all over its body, a snaky tail, and a heavy mane of hair that hung down over its fiery red eyes, almost to its nose. These creatures were said to be deadly because of poisonous plants they ate, which gave them poisonous breath. It was believed that when a Gorgon was angry or frightened it lifted its head, opened its mouth, and let out a blast of poisonous air that would cause any living creature nearby to fall to the ground, dead.

Grendel

About fifteen hundred years ago, a tale was told of the plight of King Hrothgar of Denmark, whose land lay under a terrible curse. For during the hours of darkness, a huge, shaggy figure might come lurching across the moonlit moor to the king's hall. Even though the doors were barred with stout logs, the creature would smash its way through them. One after another, terrified, shrieking men would be seized and devoured with enormous, bloody bites! When the monster had had its fill, it would turn and shamble back out into the darkness, leaving terror behind.

This horrible creature was Grendel, a savage ogre that dwelt in a dark hole in a swamp beyond the moor. No man could stand against Grendel, and it seemed that Hrothgar's people were doomed.

Then, a mighty warrior named Beowulf came from Sweden. He had heard of Grendel and vowed to slay him.

That night, when Grendel burst in, Beowulf threw himself upon the ogre. They wrestled in a titanic struggle that shook the whole hall. Finally, exerting all his strength, Beowulf tore off the monster's arm! Howling with fear and pain, Grendel rushed from the hall and staggered back to his den to die. Hrothgar and his people were free of the terror at last.

Griffin

A Griffin was a giant beast with the body, legs, and tail of a lion, and the wings and head of an eagle. However, its head, unlike an ordinary eagle's head, had two large, pointed ears. Griffins were believed to build nests high in the mountains, and their nests were said to be lined with gold that they dug from the rock with their beaks—so much gold,

Griffin

that if someone could make off with even a small amount of it, that person would be rich for life. It was told that people had tried, at times, to rob a Griffin's nest, but they usually ended up being torn to bits by the sharp claws and beaks of the savage creatures.

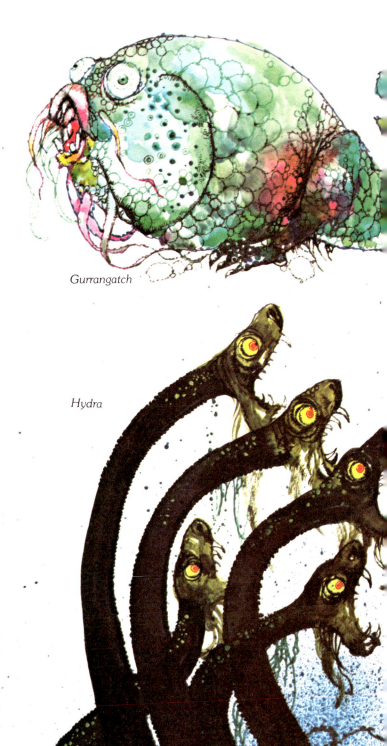

Gurrangatch

Hydra

Gurrangatch

Long ago, in the time that the first people of Australia called The Dreamtime, Gurrangatch lived in a deep, clear waterhole where two rivers came together. He was a gigantic creature, half-fish and half-reptile. One day, when Mirragen the cat man tried to catch him, Gurrangatch escaped by swimming for many miles through solid rock and so formed the channels of many new rivers. When he saw that Mirragen had followed him, Gurrangatch dived deep into the earth and stayed there.

H

Harpy

A Harpy was a nasty creature with the body and wings of a huge vulture and the head of an ugly, old witch with bears' ears. Harpies were constantly hungry and got most of their food by snatching it away from people—often, right off a table that had been set for a large dinner. Even if they left some food behind, it would be covered with filth and would have so horrible a smell that it couldn't possibly be eaten. Thus, anyone who was regularly visited by the Harpies would slowly starve! Harpies were said to have lived in ancient Greece.

Hulder Folk

The Hulder were a race of creatures reputed to live in the mountains and forests of Norway. They looked like ordinary people, but they had cowlike tails, which they tried to keep hidden whenever

they went among humans. They were fond of singing and dancing, but their songs were sad.

Hulder women were all very beautiful. They usually wore sky blue dresses and white hoods. Both Hulder men and women were anxious to marry humans, but such marriages were generally unhappy. However, if the marriage turned out to be a happy one, the Hulder's tail would slowly disappear, in time.

Hydra

The Hydra was a snakelike monster with nine heads that was said to have lived in a foggy marsh in ancient Greece. The poison of its breath spread over the nearby countryside, causing death to everyone who breathed it. The creature seemed impossible to kill, for if one of its heads was cut off, two new ones immediately grew in its place.

However, the Hydra was finally destroyed by the Greek hero Herakles (called Hercules by the Romans). Each time he cut off a head, Herakles seared the stump with a torch so that no new heads could grow. The ninth head was immortal, so to keep it from causing any trouble, Herakles buried it under a large rock.

J

Jinni

In the tan and gold deserts of the land now known as Saudi Arabia, it was said there once lived a race of beings who had lived on earth since long before there were any people. These creatures were known as Jinn, which means "hidden ones." They were shaggy beastlike things, part wolf and part hyena. They could take the forms of birds, snakes, animals, and even people, but they usually stayed invisible. Only a rooster or donkey could see a Jinni, and when they did, they would crow or bray, letting people know there was an invisible Jinni nearby.

Although Jinn were beastlike in their own form, they were clever and intelligent as humans and were skilled magicians. There were several different kinds of them, and while some were harmless and even helpful to humans, many were dangerous. They roamed the desert by night, riding on the backs of foxes, ostriches, and other

desert creatures. At dawn they vanished, returning to their own land of Jinnistan, which was a kind of Fairyland.

It was said that many Jinn were magically imprisoned in bottles and lamps by King Sulieman, a great magician.

Jotunn

Long ago, it was said among the people of Sweden, Norway, and Denmark that the Jotunns had been the first living things on earth. They were a race of giants who lived in a far northern land at the world's edge—a snowy place of vast mountains, caves, giant boulders, and great pine forests. Most resembled humans, although some, such as the eight-headed Jotunn named Starkadr, were enormous monsters.

There were several different kinds of Jotunns: frost giants, fire giants, mountain giants, and water giants. All were allied to the powers of evil and darkness and sought to destroy the Norse gods and humans. It was said Jotunns could be seen in the black, rolling clouds of thunderstorms, and their voices could be heard when thunder echoed in the mountains.

K

Kappa

Kappas were the wicked river sprites of old Japan. A Kappa was about the size of a thirteen-year-old boy. It walked upright as humans do, but it had the body and shell of a turtle, the legs of a frog, and the head of a monkey, with long, carefully trimmed hair. The top of a Kappa's head was hollow and was always filled with water, which gave the Kappa life.

Kappas delighted in drowning children who went swimming in rivers. But as Kappas were most fond of cucumbers, Japanese mothers threw cucumbers into the water to bribe the wicked creatures into sparing their children.

A warrior would sometimes seek out a Kappa and challenge it to a duel, to rid the countryside of the dangerous creature. Kappas were warlike and would gladly fight. But, being Japanese, they were naturally very polite. When the warrior bowed to it, the Kappa always bowed in return—and then the water of life would spill out of its hollow head, leaving it so weak it could be killed easily!

Kelpie

A Kelpie was a creature of Scottish legend. It usually took the form of a handsome black horse, placidly grazing on a riverbank. A Kelpie would act friendly to anyone who came by, indicating a willingness to let itself be ridden. But a person who climbed on a Kelpie's back was doomed! The creature's eyes would turn fiery red, and it would gallop straight into the river, carrying its surprised rider beneath the water to be eaten.

Kappa

However, canny Scots knew that if they could manage to slip a bridle over a Kelpie's head, the creature would become powerless and have to be an ordinary workhorse forevermore.

Khumbaba

More than three thousand years ago, the land of Sumer lay where the nation of Iraq is today. The Sumerians may have been the first people to invent a way of writing, and some of their writings tell of the giant named Khumbaba, who lived at the top of a mountain. He was said to be taller than three men, and his arms and legs were stout as tree trunks. When he walked, the earth shook as if from an earthquake. His mouth was filled with sharp teeth, there were sharp claws on his fingers and toes, and when he breathed, tongues of flame and a cyclonelike, roaring wind rushed out of his nostrils. He had one eye in the middle of his forehead, and a single glance from it would turn a person to stone!

In spite of all this, Khumbaba was slain by the great Sumerian warrior Gilgamesh.

Kobolds

The Kobolds were a race of creatures believed to live in caves and mines in the mountains of Germany. They were said to look like little deformed men with big heads. They could be dangerous to miners, for they didn't want humans to work underground. They would sometimes cause cave-ins or would carry off miners who would never be seen again.

Kraken

Kraken was a name given by Norse sailors, long ago, to a creature they greatly feared—a gigantic octopus that lived deep in the sea and sometimes rose to the surface to attack ships. The Kraken's body was said to be a good mile and a half wide,

Kraken

and its eight, snakelike arms were so thick that a man couldn't put his arms around one of them. The Kraken's eyes were wider than the length of a tall man's body and were fiery red. They glowed in darkness, and if sailors saw those twin red glows moving across the black water toward them at night, they knew they were doomed. A Kraken would wrap its huge arms around a ship and crush it like an egg! Sailors believed there were only two of these creatures in the world, and these were immortal—they would never die until the world came to an end.

For a long time, most people thought the Kraken was nothing but a legend. Today, however, we know there really are giant squids—which are octopuslike creatures—living deep in the sea. The bodies of some of them have been washed up onto beaches. None were nearly as large as the Kraken was said to be, but they were still quite big—one was seventy-four feet long with its arms stretched straight out. Many scientists think there could well be much bigger squids, and perhaps giant octopuses, too, living in the ocean's depths.

L

Lambton Worm

A legend recounts that one Sunday morning about six hundred years ago, an English knight, Sir John, the lord of Lambton, went fishing. He soon felt a tug on his line and pulled it up. He was horrified to see that he had caught a small, hideous, squirming snakelike thing. In disgust, he threw it down a nearby well.

Some time later, Sir John went off to fight in a Crusade. While he was gone, the snaky thing grew into a Worm, a snakelike dragon of enormous size. It began to come slithering out of the well at night to devour sheep, cows, or any lone human it encountered. At times, it would even smash down the wall of a cottage and eat the terrified people within. Men tried to kill the Worm, but it seemed able to withstand the blow of a sword or thrust of a spear.

When Sir John came home and found his land lying in terror of the horrible Worm, he vowed to kill the creature. He visited a wise woman who advised him to have hundreds of knife blades affixed to his armor. Following her suggestion, he went to the well and waited for the monster to come out.

Lambton Worm

The Worm tried to wrap itself around the knight and was soon bleeding from hundreds of cuts and slashes caused by the knife blades on his armor. When the creature began to weaken, Sir John hacked it to pieces.

And so, the countryside was freed from the terror. But the killing of the Worm put a dreadful curse on Sir John's family. For the next two hundred years, every one of the lords of Lambton died a violent death!

Lamia

Lamias were large, dangerous animals said to live in a sandy desert on the shore of a sea in Libya, on the North African coast. A Lamia had the head of a beautiful, long-haired woman, but the front part of its body was that of a bear, the back half was that of a goat, and it was covered with scales.

These creatures were said to be the fastest of all animals, and they got most of their food by chasing other animals down and killing them. However, a Lamia's favorite food was young men. But it didn't chase them down; it was able to attract them by means of its hissing—the only sound it could make—which apparently had a very pleasing, hypnotic effect. Charmed by the sound, men would walk right up to the Lamia—and be devoured!

Leprechaun

On quiet evenings in remote parts of Ireland not too long ago, a person might hear the faint tapping of a hammer and know that, somewhere nearby, a Leprechaun was at work, pounding nails into a tiny shoe.

Leprechauns were very small manlike creatures who were the shoemakers for the Elves and Fairies. They lived alone in secluded places, usually near an old, ruined castle. It was almost impossible for anyone to see one of them, as they could vanish in the wink of an eye if they knew a mortal was nearby.

However, if someone could manage to sneak up on a Leprechaun and grab hold of him, that person's fortune might be made. For, every Leprechaun had a hidden treasure or pot of gold, and if he were caught and held fast, he *had* to lead his captor to the treasure. But Leprechauns were incredibly quick and cunning and could usually manage to trick their captors into letting go or looking away for a moment—at which the little fellows would vanish in an instant.

Leprechauns

Leshy

Thick forests once covered many parts of Russia and other lands of eastern Europe. The people of these lands knew that in every forest there lived a Leshy.

A Leshy looked somewhat like a man, but his skin was bluish, because he had blue blood, and his long beard was green. He did not cast a shadow. His size changed depending on where he was: In the heart of the forest he was a giant with his head above the tops of the tallest trees, but at the forest's edge he became so tiny he could walk between blades of grass.

The life of a Leshy was tied to the life of the forest. In spring, when the trees budded, he was at his strongest. People might hear him laughing, shouting, or imitating the sounds of birds. If people came into the woods, the Leshy might cause them to wander around in circles for a while. But Leshies were not evil and would help the people find their way out of the woods after a time.

As summer wore on, Leshies became more quiet. By about mid-October, when the leaves were changing color, Leshies went into a deep sleep that lasted until spring.

Leshy

Loch Ness Monster

Loch Ness, a lake in northern Scotland, is about a mile wide and seven hundred feet deep. Its waters are brown and murky, and below a depth of twelve feet they are pitch black. The water is cold all year around. This deep, dark, cold lake is supposedly the home of one of the most famous of all monsters.

The Loch Ness Monster was first mentioned in a book written more than fourteen hundred years ago. According to the book, the monster attacked a man who was swimming in the lake, but it was driven off by the shouts and prayers of a monk who lived nearby.

During the next fourteen centuries the monster was apparently seen, at times, by people living near the lake, but no one in the rest of the world knew anything about it. Then, in April of 1933, a man and woman driving along the lake saw what they said looked like ''an enormous animal rolling and plunging'' in the water. Their story appeared in a newspaper.

In 1933 and 1934, a number of other people claimed to have seen the creature. An English doctor, driving along the lake, saw what he thought was the head of a strange animal poking up out of the water. He managed to take several photographs. The best of these pictures shows what looks like a long neck and small head and a bit of a broad, round back.

Over the next thirty years, more people claimed to have seen the monster, and a number of people took pictures of objects far out on the lake. None of these pictures are at all clear.

In 1967, some scientists visited the lake with special sonar equipment. (Sonar is a machine that detects things underwater by bouncing sound waves off them.) The sonar picked up what seemed to be large objects moving about deep in the lake.

In 1975, another scientist, using special equipment lowered into the lake, got some photographs of something in the depths. The pictures are fuzzy and indistinct, but one seems to show an animal with a large round body and long, snaky neck, and another shows what *could* be a close-up of a snaky head with a pair of knobby horns on it.

Many people, some of them scientists, think the Loch Ness ''Monster'' could actually be a family of creatures that have been living in the lake for thousands of years. Some people think these creatures could be plesiosaurs—long-necked, round-bodied reptiles that lived at the time of the dinosaurs, more than 70 million years ago. Some people think the creatures are giant sea slugs; some think they may be a kind of giant worm. Others think they could be a kind of long-necked seal.

But many scientists think there is no monster. They say that if creatures were living in the lake, skeletons or remains of dead ones would have been found by now. They think the photos simply show floating logs and other natural objects.

Loch Ness Monster

M

Manticore

According to the ancient Greeks, the Manticore was a dangerous animal that prowled in the forests of Asia. It had the body of a lion, the tail of a snake, and the head of a man—with neatly trimmed hair, mustache, and beard! The Manticore's mouth, however, was several times larger than a human mouth and was filled with three rows of shark's teeth.

At the end of the Manticore's serpent tail was a ball of long, needle-sharp poisonous spikes. With a snap of its tail, the beast could shoot these spikes like bullets for a distance of a hundred feet or more. There was also a poisonous stinger on the Manticore's head, hidden in its hair. A wound from either its head stinger or tail spikes caused death.

The Manticore's body was bloodred, and its roar sounded like a blend of trumpets and flutes. It

Medusa

was a flesh eater, and its favored prey was humans, which it hunted down and devoured with pleasure.

Medusa

A remote island somewhere to the west of ancient Greece was reputed to be the home of three creatures known as the Gorgons. They had the bodies of women with hideous faces, brass claws for fingernails, the teeth of hogs, and hair that was a mass of live, hissing snakes. One of these creatures, named Medusa, was so frightful that no living thing could look directly at her without being turned to stone. However, the Greek hero Perseus came upon Medusa while she was sleeping, and using a polished shield as a mirror, he was able to see Medusa without looking directly at her. He cut off her horrible head, put it into a bag, and gave it to the goddess Athena for safekeeping.

Menahune

The Menahune were a tribe of little people, the size of small children, said to have once lived in the thick forests and on the mountainsides of the

Manticore

Hawaiian Islands. They were powerful magicians who delighted in doing difficult jobs, such as making lakes and digging long irrigation canals. They could work only at night, between sunset and the first rooster crow. But every job they undertook, no matter how great, was always finished in one night—unless humans came upon them while they were working. If that happened, the Menahune vanished, and the work was left unfinished forever.

The Menahune often did work that was of great benefit to humans, and many places on the Hawaiian Islands, such as the Menahune Fishpond on Kauai, are named after them and are said to be their work.

Mermaid

For thousands of years, sailors and people living near the sea have believed in Mermaids and Mermen—creatures that lived in the sea and were human from the waist up, but fish from the waist down. Mermaids, it was said, were sometimes seen sitting on rocks near shore, combing their long golden or green hair with a comb made of fishbone, while gazing into a mirror that had been gleaned from some wrecked ship lying on the sea bottom. They sometimes sang strange, haunting songs in lovely voices. They were beautiful but dangerous, for they had power over the water. If they became angry they might cause waves that could sink ships or flood a coastal village.

Mermaids sometimes enticed young men into living with them beneath the sea. And sometimes a man could turn a Mermaid into an ordinary woman and make her his wife. This could happen if a Mermaid came ashore and a man was able to seize her comb, cloak, or some other object belonging to her. She would then have to stay with him as long as he kept the object. Some Mermaids captured in this way married men, had children,

and grew old. But, no matter how long she stayed with a man, no matter whether she had children or not, if a Mermaid could ever regain the thing that had been taken from her, she would rush to the sea, becoming a young, beautiful Mermaid again and would nevermore be seen by her husband or children.

Mermaids could sometimes apparently take on full human form by themselves and come ashore for a time. They were fond of dancing and might go into a village to join in a dance being held. But

Mermaid

villagers could usually tell that such a stranger was a Mermaid because the bottom of her dress would be dripping seawater.

Merrow

Merrows were people said to live under the sea off the coasts of Ireland. They did not actually live in the water but on a strange, dry land that was beneath the seabed itself. When they wanted to visit the land above, they used magic to pass through the water.

Merrow women were beautiful, but the men had noses like pig snouts, fiery red eyes, green hair, green teeth, and arms like short, scaly fins. Perhaps this is why Merrow women often fell in love with human men. Merrow men often formed friendships with fishermen and other people who lived near the sea.

Midgard Serpent

The people of ancient Germany, Denmark, Sweden, and Norway believed the world was an enormous circle surrounded by the waters of the sea. They called the world Midgard, meaning "Middle Abode." And they knew that in the sea around the world was the Midgard Serpent, an enormous snake that lay with its tail in its mouth and its great, scaly body forming a ring around the earth.

The Midgard Serpent's name was Jormungandr, or "Earth Monster." The threshing of its body was the cause of the great storms at sea, and the black storm clouds were its poisonous breath. It was one of the terrible creatures of evil and darkness that would someday help to destroy the earth.

Minotaur

According to legend, the Minotaur was a monster that prowled the dim corridors of a huge, sprawling

Minotaur

40

maze on the island of Crete, long ago. It had the body of a huge, muscular man, but its head was the horned, red-eyed head of a bull. It was a brutal, dull-witted creature, but even had it been clever it could never have found its way out of the incredibly complicated maze that was its prison. Anyone who wandered into that maze was lost forever.

Every nine years, seven young men and seven young women from the city of Athens, Greece, were sacrificed to the Minotaur. Soldiers forced them into the maze, where they wandered until the monster found them. What happened to them wasn't known for sure, but it was believed that the Minotaur ate them.

One year, one of those to be sacrificed was a very strong young man named Theseus. He was

Mokele-mbembe

determined to kill the Minotaur, and he had a way to escape from the maze—as he went into it, he unrolled a long piece of thread.

Within the maze, Theseus came upon the Minotaur and beat it to death with his fists. Then, he simply followed the trail of thread back out of the maze.

Mokele-mbembe

In a certain part of Cameroon, a country on the west coast of central Africa, there are said to be huge monsters known as Mokele-mbembe, which lurk in caves along riverbanks. The creatures are a kind of reptile, the size of an elephant. They have a long neck that they can twist about in all directions and a long, thick tail like that of a crocodile. Their skin is said to be smooth and grayish brown in color.

The Mokele-mbembe are not flesh eaters; they feed on plants that grow near the riverbanks. However, they are said to be very dangerous, for if people in boats come too near them, the Mokele-mbembe will smash the boats and kill the people.

There is a possibility that these creatures are not legendary, but may actually exist.

N

Nagas

The Nagas were a race of magical snake people known in the legends of India and Southeast Asia. Their home was an enormous underground kingdom called Naga-Loka—a place of beautiful parks, temples, and glittering palaces filled with treasure.

When a Naga or a Nagina (a female) came among humans, it usually took the form of an ordinary snake. But a Naga could also appear as a snake with seven heads, as a human with seven cobra hoods emerging from the neck, or as a human from the waist up and a huge, coiling snake from the waist down.

Nagas had power over the rain; they could either make it fall or keep it from falling. They often did wicked things to people, but they could also be generous and helpful. Naginas were extremely beautiful and sometimes married human men. The children of such a marriage usually became kings or nobles.

Nisse

Every house in Denmark once had a Nisse (and perhaps some still do). He looked like a very old man, the size of a young child, and wore gray clothes and a pointed cap. People usually couldn't see him, but dogs, cats, and other household animals could. Dogs, however, didn't like Nisses and would bark at them.

The Nisse looked after the house and family, coming out at night to make rounds and see that everything was all right. Most families repaid their Nisse by leaving a bowl of porridge out each night for the Nisse's supper.

Nixie

People of Germany once believed that most lakes, ponds, and rivers contained a Nixie, who lived

Nisse

Nixie

under the water in a beautiful palace. A Nixie was half-fish and half-woman, but she could take the form of a beautiful young girl or an ugly old woman. She could also make herself invisible.

Nixies were often dangerous to humans, for they sometimes kidnapped small children and sometimes lured people into deep water and drowned them. However, some Nixies fell in love with mortal men, married them, and had human children.

Nocnitsa

Mothers of babies and very young children in Russia and nearby lands once feared the Nocnitsa, a hideous old witch. They knew she might come in the night to where their child was sleeping and torture the little one by pinching or tickling it. Even worse, she might suck the child's blood.

However, it was known that the Nocnitsa couldn't stand to be near iron. So mothers often hid an iron ax or knife in the floor beneath the child's cradle to keep the Nocnitsa away.

Nuckelavee

People on the coast of Scotland once believed that on certain dark nights the Nuckelavee would come out of the sea and move about on land in search of people. It was a horrible thing to see: half-man and half-horse, but with no skin on its body, so that the white of its flesh and the red of its blood were clearly visible. Its breath was a sickening poison, and anyone the Nuckelavee breathed upon would die. However, if people could get to a stream or river before the creature caught up to them, they would be safe, for the Nuckelavee could not cross running water.

Nymph

The ancient Greeks believed that every part of a countryside was guarded by a magical being.

These beings were called Nymphs and had the appearance of pretty, young girls.

There were many kinds of Nymphs, and each kind watched over a certain sort of place. The Nymphs known as Dryads lived in, and protected, forests. Naiades lived in brooks and springs. Limoniades watched over meadows. Limniades protected marshes, and Oreades guarded mountains. Nereides lived in the sea, and Hyades lived in clouds. The Nymphs known as Hamadryads lived in oak trees, and each was actually *part* of her tree, seldom if ever leaving it. Meliades lived in fruit trees.

Nymph

43

Nymphs were happy creatures, often seen dancing and singing together. They liked mortals, and often fell in love with men. However, they would punish anyone who damaged or was disrespectful to the place or thing they guarded. They could bewitch people and make them lose their minds.

Nzangamuyo

The Nzangamuyo lived in the land of the Akamba people of eastern Kenya, Africa. It was an enormous animal, many miles long. If a man stood in one place and watched the Nzangamuyo go by, it would take four days after he saw its head for the *middle* of its body to reach him!

As the Nzangamuyo walked, the enormous, thick hairs on its long neck knocked trees aside, and its huge feet crushed big rocks to dust. Its head was flat: like a broad, thin board, but as wide as ten men standing in a row with their arms outstretched and their fingertips touching. A line of four horns sprouted from its head. Its eyes, being on top of its flat head, always looked straight up at the sky. Its mouth, too, was on the top of its head. It ate tree branches and drank by opening its mouth whenever rain fell. The Nzangamuyo's roar sounded like a peal of thunder and the hiss of falling rain.

Ogopogo

Ogopogo is the name given to a monster said to live in Lake Okanagan, in southwestern Canada. Apparently, the Indians knew of this monster long ago, and it has supposedly been seen in recent times by Canadians and Americans. Ogopogo is therefore either immortal or one of a whole family of creatures that has been living in the lake, generation after generation for centuries.

Ogopogo is said to be a snakelike creature, from thirty to seventy feet long, that can swim quite rapidly. Its head resembles the head of a goat with a shaggy beard. As far as is known, Ogopogo has never attacked anyone.

Ogre

Ogres were humanlike, flesh-eating monsters, known in many lands. They were usually big,

Ogre

burly, misshapen creatures, and many were actually giants. Their faces were generally hideous, with bloodshot eyes, a lumpy nose, and a huge mouth filled with jagged teeth. Some had two or even three heads. Ogres were hard to kill, but most were quite stupid and could easily be tricked by a clever person. Female Ogres were known as Ogresses.

See: Aigamuchab; Baba Yaga; Black Annis, Grendel; Onis; Rakshasa; Troll.

Onis

The Onis were a race of ogres of ancient Japan. They were hideous creatures with huge mouths, flat noses, and horns. They had only three fingers, three toes, and their skin was either pink, red, or bluish gray. The Onis usually carried spiked clubs.

They were often quite troublesome to people. Most of them were quite large, very strong, and fond of eating human flesh. Some, usually the red-skinned ones, enjoyed causing sickness and plagues among humans. But, like all ogres, they were stupid creatures and could usually be easily outwitted. There were simple charms and magic spells that could be used against them, and when this was done, the Onis became so enraged they could do nothing but hop about and howl, really becoming more amusing than dangerous. If their horns could be cut off, they would become quite tame.

P

Pisgie—see Pixie

Pixie

Pixies were tiny, manlike creatures with magical powers, who often came into barns and homes in England and Scotland and did useful work for people, such as threshing grain and churning butter. They seldom wore clothes, and people sometimes tried to repay Pixies for their work by making tiny garments for them. The Pixies would put the clothing on and leave, never to be seen again.

They could also be extremely mischievous. They sometimes caused dishes, silverware, candlesticks, and other objects to fly about a room and made tables and chairs chase people about. Pixies delighted in enchanting mortals so that they became hopelessly lost in an open meadow, able to see but never reach a distant road. Such people wandered aimlessly about and were said to be "Pixie-led." In Cornwall, England, Pixies were known as Pisgies. In Germany, they were called Heinzelmanchen.

Polevik

There have always been a great many wheat fields in Russia and other lands of eastern Europe, and in these fields there once lived—and perhaps still do—the creatures known as Poleviks.

A Polevik's body was the color of earth, and long, green grass grew on his head. He kept watch

Pixie

over the field in which he lived and was sometimes dangerous to humans who came into his field. He didn't bother farmers who worked in the field, of course, but if he ever found a stranger sleeping amid the grain instead of weeding or harvesting it, he was liable to strangle the intruder!

Pooka

Pookas were found only in Ireland. They generally lurked in lonely places at twilight, appearing suddenly to a farmer, milkmaid, or other lone traveler. They took the form of a horse, a mule, a donkey, a bull, a goat, or a huge dog—always coal black and with glowing red eyes. Pookas were mischievous and sometimes played pranks on people, such as suddenly rising up between their legs, carrying them off on a wild ride, then dumping them into a pond or mud puddle. Usually, Pookas' pranks were no worse than that, but a Pooka could be dangerous if the person it encountered did not treat it respectfully. However, if a person was friendly, the Pooka was usually friendly in return and might even be helpful. One of a Pooka's favorite pranks was to visit blackberry patches on Halloween night and mash all the berries flat.

R

Rakshasa

The name of this horrible creature, which was known to the Hindu people of India, means "the injurer" or "destroyer." Rakshasas were said to live in a beautiful city in the sky, where they behaved with great dignity and courtesy toward one another. But when they came among humans, whom they hated, they acted very differently. They would descend upon the earth at night, wearing hideous shapes and desiring only to cause grief, trouble, and death!

Pooka

Some Rakshasas appeared as horrible gorillalike creatures with potbellies, matted hair, and slitlike eyes. Their fingers were on their hands backward, and their fingernails were so poisonous they could cause death to any person they touched. Some Rakshasas had the heads of

46

snakes, some had several heads, some had only one eye, or one leg, or many legs.

There were several different kinds of these creatures, known by different names and with different ways of troubling people. Pisachas were bloodthirsty horrors who lurked in cemeteries and ate the bodies of the dead. Bhuts ate dead bodies too, but they could also enter dead bodies and make them stalk into villages, causing terror, destroying things, and murdering the inhabitants. Grahas could take over the bodies of living people, bringing dreadful diseases to them or driving them mad. All the Rakshasas could also take the forms of ordinary men and women and use these disguises for making mischief.

But, despite their powers, Rakshasas were quite stupid and could often easily be tricked. If a man found himself confronted by a threatening Rakshasa, he had only to call it "Uncle" and act as if they were related. Confused and puzzled, the Rakshasa would let him go, unharmed.

Roc

Rakshasa

Roc

Rocs, also known as Rukhs, were gigantic birds appearing in the legends of the Middle East and India. So huge were these birds that one in flight blotted out the sun and made a great shadow, dark as night, upon the land below. It was said that a single feather from a Roc's wing was as much as ninety spans—about sixty-seven feet—long.

When the Arabian sailor and storyteller Sindbad was cast ashore on the isle of the Rocs, he came upon a Roc egg he at first thought was a large, domed building. He saw female Rocs bringing

47

food to their babies, just as ordinary-sized birds do—only, the food that mother Rocs brought their young was elephants!

Rusalka

In Russia, long ago, only a very foolish man would walk near a lake or river late at night. A Rusalka might be lurking beneath the dark water. A Rusalka looked like an ugly girl with a thin, gray body, tangled hair, and glowing green eyes. With an evil laugh she would leap from the water to seize a man in a grip strong as iron and drag him into the water to drown.

These evil creatures were thought to be the ghosts of girls who had drowned and who were doomed to haunt the lake or river where they had died. They became wicked creatures who not only sought to drown people but delighted in causing all kinds of trouble as well. Rusalkas would tear holes in the nets fishermen cast into the water and would break dikes to cause floods. They could make torrents of rain fall on a farmer's fields to damage the crops.

Rusalkas stayed in the water through fall, winter, and spring. In the summer, they climbed up into birch or weeping willow trees that hung over the water. At night, they could sometimes be heard calling to one another in evil voices. Their green eyes could sometimes be seen glowing among the leaves.

S

Sasabonsam

The Ashanti people of the African country of Ghana once believed in a forest creature called Sasabonsam. He was a hairy giant with long legs, bloodred eyes, and feet on both sides of his ankles. He would stand hidden among the trees, and when an Ashanti hunter passed beneath him, Sasabonsam would scoop the man up with a foot and eat him.

Satyr

Ancient Greeks believed that Satyrs lived in forests and on wooded mountainsides. A Satyr had the upper body of a man, but the legs and hoofs of a goat. His face was goatlike, with a slanting forehead, flat nose, and wide mouth. Horns sprouted from his forehead, and he whisked a little goat tail.

Satyrs were wild, rather lazy creatures that spent their time dancing, making music with flutes and drums, playing with Nymphs, and looking for

Satyr

other ways to amuse themselves. They were shy and usually kept away from mortals except to play tricks on them.

Seal People

The Seal People were well known in Iceland, Scotland, Ireland, and other places with coasts washed by the cold waters of the North Atlantic. In Scotland, these creatures were known as Roane.

The Seal People looked like ordinary seals when they were swimming in the sea. But at times they came onto land, removed their sealskins, and had the bodies of humans. In the Faeroe Islands it was said that every nine days the Seal People came ashore to a hidden place and held a night-long dance.

A number of human men became husbands of Seal women, for if a man found the sealskin one of these women had taken off, she had to become his wife and stay with him if he wished it. However, if the woman could ever regain her sealskin, she would put it on and return to the water as a seal, leaving her husband and children behind forever.

Sea Serpent

More than twenty-three hundred years ago, the great Greek scientist Aristotle wrote of gigantic serpents said to have attacked ships off the coast of Libya in the waters of the Mediterranean Sea. Since then, creatures believed to be Sea Serpents have been seen many times.

They were apparently seen often in northern waters by sailors from Sweden, Norway, and Denmark. In 1539, the archbishop of Uppsala, Sweden, wrote a book in which he described a creature Swedish sailors had seen. He said it was black, covered with scales, and had "flaming, shining eyes." It was some 200 feet long and 20 feet wide.

A little more than two hundred years later, the

Sea Serpent

bishop of Bergen, Norway, also wrote a book of stories he had been told by sailors about Sea Serpents they had seen. One of the stories described a Serpent seen in 1746. It had a horselike head, a long white mane, and black eyes.

In 1817, a great many people saw what looked like an enormous snake with a humped back swimming in and around Gloucester Harbor in Massachusetts. And in 1848, many of the officers and men of the British warship H.M.S. *Daedalus* saw what appeared to be a giant Serpent swim past their ship as they sailed around the southern tip of Africa. The creature was dark brown, with a snakelike head and a thick mane.

These are just a few of the many reports of Sea Serpents. Many people feel, however, that all the ''Sea Serpents'' that have been sighted were actually commonplace objects such as floating seaweed, or large sharks, whales, or fish. But, many other people feel there really is a family of rare, unknown, serpentlike creatures living in the ocean, but that these creatures may *not* be giant snakes. Some people think the ''Sea Serpent'' could actually be a kind of huge, long-necked seal, an extremely large giant sea otter, or a whale of a kind that lived millions of years ago and was thought to be extinct.

Sirens

Ancient Greek sailors dreaded voyages that took them among the islands lying between Italy and the island of Sicily. The sailors feared they might encounter the Sirens, and that would surely be the death of them. The Sirens were said to be a group of creatures that had the upper body of a woman and the lower body of a bird. (Some people said they had the lower body of a fish.) They supposedly lived on one of the islands, and on sighting a ship they would begin to sing in voices so incredibly beautiful that a man would forget everything

and desire only to stay near the Sirens and listen to them forever. The beach of their island was said to be thickly strewn with the bones of sailors who had come ashore and eventually died because they were too enchanted even to think about eating or drinking.

The Sirens were outwitted by the Greek Odysseus. Knowing his ship had to pass their island, he stuffed up the ears of his men so that they couldn't hear the singing. Then he had himself tied to the ship's mast so that he would be able to hear the Sirens' song but wouldn't be able to go to them. Thus, he became the only man ever to hear the singing of the Sirens and live to tell about it.

Siren

Snow Woman

Long ago in Japan, it was said that a cold, weary traveler, trudging along on a winter night, far from any house or village, might suddenly behold a woman standing before him in the snow. Her beautiful, pale face gleamed in the cold starlight, and she held out arms as white as the snow itself, promising to warm the traveler with her embrace. Few men could resist this lovely creature, but if a man let her hug him, he was doomed. The woman was the terrible Snow Woman, and her touch was death. When her arms went around a man, he would feel as if he were getting warmer. But, in reality, life was draining out of him. Days later, people would find his frozen body lying in the snow.

Sphinx

Legend tells that the city of Thebes, in ancient Greece, was once troubled by a monster known as the Sphinx, which had the body of a lion and the head of a woman. The Sphinx would crouch beside the main road into Thebes and wait for travelers. She stopped everyone who tried to pass and demanded the answer to this riddle: ''What animal goes on four feet in the morning, on two feet at noon, and on three feet in the evening?'' If the traveler couldn't give the right answer—and none could—the Sphinx ate him.

However, one day the Sphinx stopped a young man named Oedipus and put her question to him. Oedipus thought for a time and then replied: ''The answer is a man. As a baby, in the morning of his life, he crawls on all fours. When he is grown up, in the noon of his life, he walks on two legs. And when he is old and bent, in the evening of his life, he goes on three supports—his two legs plus a cane.''

The Sphinx was so enraged that she hurled herself off a cliff and was killed.

Sphinx

Su

A few hundred years ago, people of Europe believed that strange beasts called Su lived in South America. A Su had the body of a lion, the front legs of a tiger, the back legs of a wolf, and the head of a woman—with a beard! Its tail was like a huge, furry plume, and it was said that a female Su often carried her babies on her back, holding the great tail over them like an umbrella to protect them from rain and wind.

Sukuyan

In Trinidad, in the West Indies, if a woman came to someone's house and asked to borrow either some salt or matches, most people knew better than to give her what she asked for. They knew she might well be a Sukuyan—a vampire! And, if they gave her either salt or matches, she would then have the power to come into their home at night and suck their blood as they slept! However, if they refused her, or if they put a cross in the window, she was powerless to enter.

Swan Maiden

In many lands, stories are told of how a young man, passing a quiet pond in a forest glade, would see a lovely white swan gliding toward the grassy bank. Admiring the bird's beauty, the man would hide behind a tree to watch for a time. He would be amazed to see the swan remove its feathers and become a beautiful young girl—a Swan Maiden.

The girl would go into the water to bathe, and the man would pick up the feather cape she had left lying in the grass. This would give him power over the maiden. If he demanded that she become his wife, she had to do so.

Sometimes, say the stories, the man would also have to make a certain promise. As long as he did not break the promise and kept the feather cloak hidden, the girl would stay with him and he was gloriously happy. But, if he broke the promise, or if she were able to find the cloak and put it on, she would again become a swan and would soar off into the sky, never to be seen by him again.

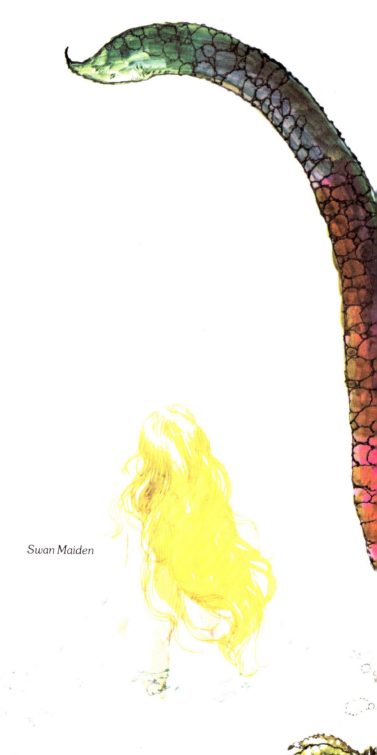

Swan Maiden

T

Tapio

Tapio was said to live in the great forest that once spread over part of ancient Finland. Most of the time he was invisible, but he could take the form of a man with a dark beard who wore a fur cap and a cloak made of tree moss. He often showed himself to people who were lost in the forest and led them out. If they were hunters, he might help them to find deer and other game. But sometimes people made Tapio angry, and then he would cause them to dance among the trees until they died.

Tarasque

According to legend, the people of the town of Nerluc, in France, once lived in terror of a winged, scaly dragon known as the Tarasque. The creature had come swimming up the Rhône River from the east and made its home in a forest on the riverbank near the town. It preyed on unwary travelers making their way through the forest, and when there wasn't enough of them, it would stalk into Nerluc and make a meal off the first person it encountered. Sixteen of the town's sturdiest and bravest men tried to kill the beast, but it killed eight of them and drove the rest to flight.

The Tarasque was finally conquered by a famous holy woman, Saint Martha. She sprinkled the beast with holy water, which made it harmless and tame, then led it into the town where the people beat it to death with clubs. The town took the name of Tarascon as a reminder that it once had the distinction of being preyed upon by the terrible Tarasque.

Tengu

The Tengu were magical beings that lived deep in forests and high on mountains in ancient Japan. A Tengu resembled a tall, sturdy man, but it had reddish skin and an enormously long red nose, or

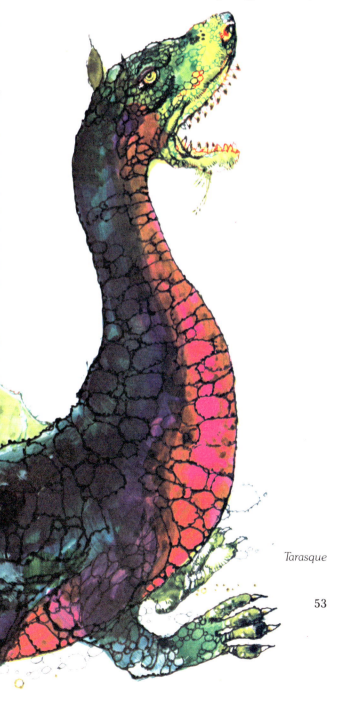

Tarasque

53

sometimes a nose that resembled the beak of a large bird. Each Tengu carried a magic fan made from a leaf of the yatsude tree. The fan gave the Tengu the power to fly.

The Tengu had servants known as Crow Tengu. These were small creatures with human bodies and the wings of birds. Instead of a nose and mouth, however, a Crow Tengu had a bird's beak. Its fingernails and toenails were like a tiger's claws, and its eyes were perfectly round and glowed with light as bright as a flash of lightning.

Tengu were fond of playing tricks on humans. They could cause rain, windstorms, and volcanic eruptions. They were expert swordsmen and sometimes taught the art of swordplay to young Japanese warriors.

Once, nearly a thousand years ago, they taught the art of swordplay to a young man named Ushiwaku-maru. He became the greatest swordsman in Japan and helped his brother Yorotomo Minamoto become the first shogun, or highest ruler of all Japan.

Thunderbird

Many Indian tribes throughout North America knew that the sound of thunder was caused by the flapping wings of the Thunderbird, an eaglelike bird so enormous that it darkened the whole sky as it flew high above the earth. The rain during a thunderstorm was water spilling from a huge lake on the bird's back. Lightning was caused by the blinking of the bird's eyes.

The Haida, Tlingits, and other tribes of Alaska and the northwest coast believed the Thunderbird was actually a giant man who lived high in the mountains and who owned a winged cape made of feathers. When he was hungry, he put on the cape and became the Thunderbird, flying in search of food. The food he sought was whales, which he swallowed down whole!

Torch

The Torch lived near the Black Sea in western Armenia, a land that is now part of the Soviet Union. He was thought to be a giant with a huge, rather lumpy body and an extremely ugly face. He was immensely strong and could crush rocks to dust with his bare hands. He could also smooth boulders into flat slabs by rubbing them with his palm and would then chisel pictures on them with his thumbnail!

Thunderbird

Once, many warriors came in ships to capture the giant. The angry Torch chased the men back to their ships, and as they frantically tried to sail away, he tore up nearby hills and threw them at the ships, sinking several.

Triton

Tritons were often seen, it was said, in the sea around ancient Greece. They were men from the waist up, but from the waist down they had the scaly, finned body of a fish. Their teeth were sharp, and they had claws instead of fingernails. They were wild, noisy creatures, constantly blowing on trumpets made of large seashells and yelling in loud, savage voices.

Some Tritons had a pair of horse legs and could walk on land. One of these wild creatures came ashore near the town of Tanagra and caused a great deal of trouble. The people finally got rid of him by placing a large jar of wine on the beach. The Triton drank the wine and fell asleep, upon which some of the villagers put him to death.

Troll

Most people who lived long ago in Norway, Sweden, and Denmark wouldn't have dared walk through a forest at night. They believed that was when Trolls prowled. Trolls looked like huge, burly, misshapen men and women, but they weren't human—their bodies were formed out of mountain rock. They were filthy creatures, often so covered with dirt that plants and moss grew on them. Some of the biggest Trolls, who were truly gigantic, even had trees growing out of the thick soil that was matted into the hair on their heads!

Trolls were dangerous. At the very least, they might carry a human off to be their slave. And at worst, a Troll might eat its human catch. There were small Trolls as well as big ones, but these small Trolls were dangerous too. A crowd of them

Troll

could overpower even a strong man and carry him off.

Trolls, however, were very dull-witted and easily tricked. If they could be kept from getting back to their caves before sunrise, they were doomed. Daylight would turn them into lumps of lifeless stone.

U

Unicorn

The Unicorn was known throughout Europe, Asia, and parts of Africa. It was believed to be a horselike animal with a single horn on its forehead. The ancient Greeks described it as a white horse with a purple head, blue eyes, and a long horn that was white at the bottom, black in the middle, and red at the top. In China, where the unicorn was known as a Ki-lin, it had the body of a deer, the hoofs of a horse, and the tail of an ox. Its voice was like a deep bell.

The people of medieval Europe knew the Unicorn as a pure white horse with a goatlike beard, a lion's tail, an ox's hoofs, and a long spiraled horn. It lived in deserts and on high mountains. It was incredibly swift and could not be caught by hunters or traps. It could only be captured by a young, unmarried girl. If she would wait alone in a forest, a Unicorn would come and lay its head in her lap, then tamely follow her, wherever she went.

The horn of a Unicorn had special power. If a snake poisoned the water of the animals' drinking pool in the forest, the Unicorn would stir the water with its horn and the poison would disappear. Kings, nobles, and wealthy merchants were willing to pay a fortune for a wine cup made from a Unicorn's horn. Such a cup, it was said, would change color if poison was added to it, warning the owner not to drink.

56

V

Vampire

Nighttime brought fear to the countrysides of Hungary, Rumania, and other parts of the Balkans. For it was well known there that during the hours of darkness the terrible creatures known as

Vampire

Vampires came forth to seek the blood of humans. A Vampire was a dead person whose body had been taken over by an evil spirit. By day, the body lay in a hidden place as if dead, resting upon earth. With the setting of the sun, the Vampire arose. Keeping its human form, or perhaps taking the form of a bat, it went in search of the blood it needed. It attacked sleeping people, sucking their blood without awakening them, but causing them to have dreadful nightmares and to grow weak and listless. Unfortunately, people bitten by a Vampire often became Vampires themselves.

There were a number of ways in which people could protect themselves against a Vampire's attack. Sprays of fresh garlic or bulbs of dried garlic, bells, or objects made of iron placed at a door or window would prevent a Vampire from entering a house. After the Balkans became Christianized, a cross or crucifix would also protect against Vampires. If a Vampire's body could be found, the creature could be destroyed by driving a wooden stake through its heart and burning the corpse to ashes.

See: Azeman; Sukuyan; Vetāla.

Vetāla

Graveyards in India were the abode of Vetālas—creatures that sometimes appeared as men with their hands and feet turned backward and their hair standing on end. A Vetāla might only be mischievous, delighting in frightening people or playing tricks on them. But some Vetālas were vampires, who sought human blood to drink.

Vodyanoi

A Vodyanoi was a water creature that lived in a lake, pond, or stream in Russia and other eastern European lands. No one knew exactly what a Vodyanoi looked like, because it could change its shape. It might appear as a huge fish covered with

moss, as a giant man covered with moss, as an old man with long green hair and a green beard, or as a man with glowing red eyes and paws instead of hands.

Each Vodyanoi lived beneath the water in a palace made of gold, silver, and glass. The palace was lighted by a magic stone that glowed more brightly than the sun. A Vodyanoi would stay in its palace during the day and would come out at night to move about in the water.

These creatures were very dangerous to humans. If a Vodyanoi caught anyone bathing or

Vodyanoi

swimming, or even standing near the water's edge, he would pull the person into the water to drown. A drowned person became a Vodyanoi's slave forever, for a Vodyanoi did not die. Each month, when the moon went from a sliver to a full circle, the Vodyanoi would grow older. But in the second half of the month, when the moon went back to a sliver, the Vodyanoi grew young again.

W

Wakonyingo

Inside the very top of Mount Kilimanjaro, the highest mountain in Africa (in the country of Tanzania) there was a little world, or so it was believed, where the Wakonyingos lived. They were little people, no bigger than young children, but with extremely large heads. In fact, their heads were so large that they had to sleep sitting up, for if they were to lie down, they were too top-heavy to get up again! Thus, if a Wakonyingo fell down, he had to just lie there until some of his friends happened by. For this reason, every Wakonyingo carried a horn with which to blow a call for help if necessary.

The world of the Wakonyingos was thought to be much like the world outside—with groves of banana trees, grassy plains where herds of cattle grazed, and a small village. Humans could reach it by going through a door at the top of the mountain and climbing a tall ladder. The Wakonyingos were kindly little creatures willing to give magical help to people who were in need. However, if someone mistook them for children, their feelings were hurt and they would refuse to give any help.

Washer at the Ford

A man walking through a moonlit forest in Scotland comes to a ford in a stream—-a narrow, shallow place where a person can easily cross to the

other side without getting more than his legs wet. But, the man stops short with a gasp of dismay, for there is a figure kneeling by the water. It is the figure of a little, old woman, and she is washing some garments in the stream.

Slowly, the man moves nearer. It is as he feared! He can see that the garments the woman is wash-

ing are filled with blood that spreads out into the stream. Then, the woman turns to look at him. She has only one nostril and one tooth that sticks straight out of her mouth. He sees that her bare feet, sticking out of her black skirt, are webbed!

It is the Washer at the Ford, and the man trembles with dread. He knows that if the woman flicks one of the bloody garments at him it means he is soon to die violently—by sword, spear, ax, or poison!

The Washer at the Ford appeared only to foretell someone's death. However, the person who saw her was not necessarily the one who was to die—he might be a friend or relative of the doomed one. In that case, if he could catch hold of the Washer, she would have to reveal the name of the person whose death she was foretelling. She would also have to grant her captor three wishes.

Wendigo

Wendigoes were manlike giants of horrible appearance that roamed the forests of northeastern North America where the Chippewa, Algonquin, and other tribes lived. They could walk on water and from a distance might look like a towering black cloud moving across a lake or over the land. They were eaters of human flesh and would usually snatch up any human they encountered, gulping down flesh and crunching bones!

The Indians knew that a man could become a Wendigo. A hunter lost in the woods, getting hungrier and hungrier, would begin to act like an animal. The spirit of the wild would enter him, and he would seek human flesh to appease his hunger.

Werewolf

People in many parts of Europe knew of, and feared, Werewolves—humans who could take on the form of a wolf and prowl the night in search of people to attack and devour. Werewolves were doubly dangerous because they had the speed, savagery, and sharp teeth of a wolf, as well as the intelligence and cunning of a human.

Some Werewolves were unfortunate people who had been bewitched or cursed and could not help themselves. Although they hated it, they had to become wolves at night. But most Werewolves were evil magicians who were able to change themselves by putting on the skin of a wolf. At daybreak, the magician would remove the

Washer at the Ford

Werewolf

wolfskin and hide it, becoming human once again. It was said that if the skin was hidden in a cold place, the Werewolf would shiver all day. Thus, a person who shivered on a warm day was known to be a Werewolf.

A Werewolf would die if the hidden skin was found and destroyed. But the Werewolf could not be killed by any weapon except one made of silver. It could be wounded by an ordinary weapon, however, and any wound it received while it was in wolf form would also appear on its human body. Many a tale is told of someone who bravely cut off the paw of a savage wolf that attacked him in the night and who discovered the next day that a neighbor had mysteriously lost a hand!

In parts of the world where there were no wolves, it was believed that people could take on the forms of other animals. In Southeast Asia, people feared Weretigers; in Africa, it was whispered that some people could become leopards; in Japan, it was said there were those who could become foxes; and in South America, many of the Indian tribes believed certain magicians could become jaguars.

Whowie

Whowie supposedly roamed part of Australia long ago, when only the people now known as Aborigines lived there. He was a terrifying creature

Werewolf

60

with the body of an enormous lizard, the head of a huge frog, and six legs. He lived in a vast, underground cavern, from which many long tunnels led up to a riverbank.

At night, Whowie would crawl up one of the tunnels and creep along the riverbank in search of food. He ate kangaroos, wallabies, and wombats, but he preferred humans—by the dozens! When Whowie came upon a camp of sleeping people, he would quietly swallow them whole, one after another. He once ate an entire tribe, except for one small boy who awoke in time and ran away.

Finally, all the tribes of the region banded together to kill the monster. They plugged up all the tunnels to his cave but one, and in the entrance of that one, they built an enormous fire. Soon, they could hear Whowie coughing and roaring as he tried to escape from the smoke-filled cave. By the time he discovered that the only way out was through the fire, he was weak from breathing so much smoke, and he burned himself badly dragging his huge body through the flames. At once, hundreds of men attacked him with clubs and spears. He was too weak and hurt to put up much of a fight, and they were finally able to kill him.

However, it is said that Whowie's ghost now haunts the underground cavern. Sometimes, when the wind blows through the riverbank tunnels, his roaring can be faintly heard.

Wild Hunt

A person walking through a lonely part of the English countryside after dark might suddenly hear a noise sweeping through the sky—a faint, wild tumult like the distant barking and baying of a pack of hounds, high above the ground. Then, the person had better crouch down and try to hide, for those sounds would mean the Wild Hunt was drawing near, and the lone traveler might become its quarry!

Whowie

Zombi

The Wild Hunt was a pack of ghostly hounds. Some people said these hounds were black, with fire red eyes; others said they were snow-white, with red ears and eyes like silver mirrors. They moved with the speed of the wind, and running among them was the shadowy figure of a man with horns or branching antlers on his head. Once the hunter and his hounds sighted a person, that person was doomed.

The hounds of the Wild Hunt were also known as Gabriel Hounds, Ratchet (Racket) Hounds, and Ghost Hounds.

Wild Hunt

Z

Zombi

People of Haiti, an island in the West Indies, feared to be out in a lonely place at night. They were afraid they might see a figure coming slowly toward them—a gaunt, human figure, with staring eyes, moving with a slow, stiff shuffle. A Zombi!

A Zombi was a person whose soul was stolen by an evil magician or witch and who then seemed to die. But after the person was buried, the magician would dig up the body and bring it back to life to be a slave. A Zombi could see and move, but it could not think for itself. It could only do the bidding of its magician master, who might put it to endless work, or far worse, send it out at night to rob and murder!

In Jamaica and other parts of the West Indies, these creatures are known as Jumbies.

Pronunciation Guide

Abatwa ah-BAH-twah
Abiku ah-BEE-koo
Abominable Snowman
  uh-BAHM-nuh-buhl
  SNOH-man
Acheri ah-SHEHR-ee
Ahuizotl ah-hwee-ZOHT-l
Aigamuchab eye-guh-MOO-
  chahb
Al ahl
Ankou ANG-koo
Arwe ahr-way
Azeman ahz-MAHN
Baba Yaga BAH-bah YAH-
  gah
Banshee BAN-shee
Basilisk BAS-uh-lisk
Bay-kok BAY-kawk
Black Annis BLAK ANN-niss
Bodach buh-THAHK
Bogeyman BUG-ee-man
Boggart BAWG-uhrt
Brownie BROW-nee
Bunyip BUHN-yihp
Centaur SEN-tawr
Chimera ky-MIHR-uh
Clurican KLUHR-ih-kahn
Cockatrice KAHK-uh-truhs
Cyclops SY-klahps
Dogai duh-GUY
Domovoi doh-moh-VOY
Fafnir FAHV-nuhr
Fay FAY
Fenris FEHN-rihs
Fomorians foh-WAWR-ih-ans
Ghoul GOOL
Gigantes gih-GAHN-tayes
Gnome NOHM

Goblin GAHB-luhn
Golem GOH-luhm
Goo-Teekhl goo-TEE-kuhl
Gorgon GAWR-guhn
Grendel GREHN-duhl
Griffin GRIHF-uhn
Gurrangatch guhr-uhn-
  GATCH
Harpy HAHR-pee
Hulder HUHL-der
Hydra HY-druh
Jinni JEE-nee
Jotunn YAW-tun
Kappa KAP-a
Kelpie KEHL-pee
Khumbaba koom-BAH-buh
Kobolds KOH-bawlds
Kraken KRAHK-uhn
Lambton Worm LAM-tuhn
  WUHRM
Lamia LAY-mee-uh
Leprechaun LEHP-ruh-kahn
Leshy LEH-shih
Loch Ness LAHK NEHS
Manticore MAN-tih-kohr
Medusa mih-DOO-suh
Menahune mehn-eh-HYOO-
  nee
Mermaid MUHR-mayd
Merrow MEHR-oh
Midgard MIHD-gahrd
Minch MIHNCH
Minotaur MIHN-uh-tawr
Mokele-mbembe moh-KEE-
  lee-em-behm-bee
Naga NAH-gah
Nisse NIHS-eh
Nixie NIHK-sih

Nocnitsa nawk-NEET-zuh
Nuckelavee nuk-luh-VEEH
Nymph NIHMF
Nzangamuyo en-zahn-gah-
  MOO-yoh
Ogopogo oh-goh-POH-goh
Ogre OH-guhr
Oni OH-nee
Pisgie PIHZ-gee
Pixie PIHK-see
Polevik pohl-eh-VEEK
Pooka POO-kah
Rakshasa RAHK-sha-sa
Roc RAHK
Rusalka ruh-SAL-kuh
Sasabonsam sah-suh-BAHN-
  suhm
Satyr SAYT-uhr
Sirens SY-ruhns
Sphinx SFIHNGS
Su SOO
Sukuyan soo-koo-YAHN
Tapio TAH-pee-oh
Tarasque ta-RAHSK
Tengu TEHN-ngu
Triton TRYT-n
Troll TROHL
Unicorn YOO-nuh-kawrn
Vampire VAM-pyr
Vetala vuh-TAHL-uh
Vodyanoi vohd-yah-NOY
Wakonyingo wah-kuhn-
  YING-goh
Wendigo WEHN-dih-goh
Werewolf WIHR-wulf
Whowie hwoo-WEE
Yeti YEHT-ee
Zombie ZAHM-bee

Tom McGowen

Known for both his science and fiction writing, Tom McGowen has many books for children to his credit. His popular *Album* series for Rand McNally includes *Album of Astronomy, Album of Whales, Dinosaurs and Other Prehistoric Animals, Album of Dinosaurs, Album of Sharks, Album of Reptiles,* and *Album of Rocks and Minerals.* Mr. McGowen applies his penchant for research and detail to the realm of fiction as well and has authored several fantasies for children.

In *Encyclopedia of Legendary Creatures,* he combines his talents to produce a delightful and well-researched volume describing more than a hundred creatures of myth and legend. The book also marks his first collaboration with Victor Ambrus.

Mr. McGowen is an editor of materials for children.

He is married and the father of a son and three daughters.

Victor G. Ambrus

Victor Ambrus is an illustrator of international repute. He has worked for many publishers in the United States and Britain and has illustrated over three hundred books. He has twice won the Kate Greenaway Medal: in 1965 for his book *The Three Poor Tailors* and for his work throughout the year; and in 1975 for *Horses in Battle* and *Mishka,* which he wrote and illustrated.

Mr. Ambrus studied at the Hungarian Academy of Fine Art and went on to the Royal College of Art in London where he was the Royal Scholar in 1959. He is a Fellow of the Royal Society of Arts and teaches in England at the West Surrey College of Art, where he is Visiting Lecturer.

The handsomely illustrated *Encyclopedia of Legendary Creatures* is Mr. Ambrus's third work for Rand McNally. Previously he illustrated *Robin Hood* and *Favorite Tales from Shakespeare.*

64